The Kite

Note

Once a reader can recognize and identify the 20 words used to tell this story, he or she will be able to read successfully the entire book. These 20 words are repeated throughout the story, so that young readers will be able to easily recognize the words and understand their meaning.

The 20 words used in this book are:

birds	I	my	so
clouds	if	on	the
could	in	ride	touch
fly	it	see	trees
high	kite	sky	will

Library of Congress Cataloging-in-Publication Data
Packard, Mary.
    The kite / by Mary Packard; illustrated by Benrei Huang.
      p.   cm.—(My first reader)
    Summary: A child watches his kite fly high in the sky.
      Previously published by Grolier.
      ISBN 0-516-05355-8
      (1. Kites—Fiction. 2. Stories in rhyme.) I. Huang, Benrei,
ill. II. Title. III. Series.
PZ8.3.P125K1 1990
(E)—dc20

90-30157
CIP
AC

The Kite

Written by Mary Packard   Illustrated by Benrei Huang

CP CHILDRENS PRESS®
CHICAGO

Text © 1990 Nancy Hall, Inc. Illustrations © Benrei Huang.
All rights reserved. Published by Childrens Press®, Inc.
Printed in the United States of America. Published simultaneously in Canada.
Developed by Nancy Hall, Inc. Designed by Antler & Baldwin Design Group.

3 4 5 6 7 8 9 10 R 99 98 97 96 95 94

See my kite.

7

See it fly, fly, fly.

See it fly so high.

See it fly in the sky.

Will it touch the trees?

14

Will it touch the birds?

Will it touch the clouds?

Will it touch the sky?

See my kite.

See it fly so high.

If I could ride on my kite,

27

I could fly, fly, fly.